How Is Hyperemesis Gravidarum

STEFANIE SYBENS & SARAH TITMUS

Copyright © 2021 Stefanie Sybens & Sarah Titmus

All rights reserved.

ISBN: 9798737400132

DEDICATION

We want to thank all the ladies who submitted their story. You are all warriors and extremely brave for opening yourself up and showing the world what it's like to suffer from Hyperemesis Gravidarum.

We also want to thank the Real Birth Project for writing affirmations specifically for HG sufferers.

Lastly, our own Sarah Titmus wrote the lovely poems for this book which has given it so much more depth. If you want to have your own poem created, or read more of her work, please give her a follow on Facebook and Instagram @sarahTwrites

INTRODUCTION

Nausea and Vomiting in pregnancy affects up to 80% of pregnant women and is one of the most common reasons for hospital admissions during pregnancies. Hyperemesis Gravidarum is a severe form of Nausea and Vomiting in Pregnancy, which affects roughly 0.3–3.6% of pregnant women. It is mainly characterised by severe nausea and vomiting associated with weight loss of more than 5% of pre-pregnancy weight, dehydration and electrolyte imbalances.[1]

HG reduces quality of life, it makes the woman's ability to function on a day-to-day basis nearly impossible and it can negatively impact relationships with her partner and family. Women may experience grief for loss of a normal pregnancy and may have to take absence from work, which will often cause financial pressures. They can feel very isolated and that doctors are reluctant to treat the condition.

Stefanie and Sarah have both suffered with Hyperemesis Gravidarum during their pregnancies. They are extremely passionate about raising awareness and sharing their stories.

Stefanie is an author and the founder of HG & early

---

[1] Dr M Shehmar MRCOG, Birmingham; Dr MA MacLean MRCOG, Kilmarnock, Scotland;
Professor C Nelson-Piercy FRCOG, FRCP, London; Dr R Gadsby, University of Warwick, Coventry; and Dr M O'Hara, Patient Representative (Pregnancy Sickness Support). "The Management of Nausea and Vomiting of Pregnancy and Hyperemesis Gravidarum." *RCOG*, June 2016, https://www.rcog.org.uk/globalassets/documents/guidelines/green-top-guidelines/gtg69-hyperemesis.pdf

motherhood and Sarah is a passionate poet and a volunteer for Pregnancy Sickness Support.

They started talking about launching a book together that would contain HG stories. They wanted the book to be used as a tool for current HG sufferers and as a processing step for former HG sufferers. They have gathered stories from all around the world and the stories cover a variety of heartfelt topics including; HPV, mental health, suicidal thoughts, termination and pregnancy after loss.

Stefanie & Sarah

Each moment is one closer

THE HG STORY OF...
STEFANIE

The sickness found its way into my body when I was five weeks pregnant. It took over every fibre of my being and there was nothing I could do about it. My GP gave me Metoclopramide pre-emptively but it didn't work. I went to EPU (Early Pregnancy Unit) when I was 5.5 weeks pregnant where they administered fluids and gave me a cocktail of Metoclopramide, Cyclizine and Ondansetron. That still didn't keep the sickness at bay so they kept me overnight. I was so happy when they released me the next day because I was feeling better but as soon as I got home, I started vomiting again. 30 times a day. Easily. A week had already passed with me not keeping anything in and I just felt lifeless.

My heart rate went up to 180

I went to A&E the next evening because I couldn't take it anymore. I had to wait six hours to be seen. I remember letting myself fall on the dirty, wet bathroom floor because I couldn't stand up anymore. I felt so weak that dying didn't seem too bad anymore. I thought I would feel better when they finally offered me a Cyclizine injection, but I developed an allergic reaction right after. I started to feel incredibly warm, drops of sweat were falling off my body and my heart started to race. I knew something wasn't right. My heart rate went up to 180 and I was shaking uncontrollably. Healthcare professionals started to gather around me, looking worried, and did an ECG. That's all I can remember.

I woke up in a hospital bed on the gynaecology unit. I couldn't believe everything that had happened the past week. There was so much fear and I was only six weeks pregnant. Someone from the medical obstetric unit came and saw me and prescribed me Metoclopramide, Ondansetron and Stemetil, another new combination to try, and send me back home. I was feeling hopeful… until the same thing happened. As soon as I got back home, I started vomiting again. The vomiting wasn't the worst part though, it was the constant sickness that wouldn't leave you alone.

I couldn't even remember my name

I received a follow-up appointment the next week when I would be 6.5 weeks pregnant. I'll never forget that week. I couldn't eat or drink anything ever since I was five weeks pregnant and I felt like I was dying. I couldn't think straight anymore, sometimes couldn't even remember my name and I was longing to be able to drink a bit, but I couldn't. Sleep had become impossible as well because of the sickness and my heart was pounding constantly.

I don't know how I made it to this appointment. I remember holding a vomit bag in front of me in the taxi and while walking to the antenatal clinic. I had to stop twice in the hospital to vomit and when I reached reception, the woman behind it said that I wasn't looking too good. When we were finally seen, I explained how I had been feeling and they ensured me that there were other medication to try but I said I couldn't do this anymore. I couldn't feel like this for another nine months. I felt like I was dying… and I didn't want to. They got the head consultant who I had seen for pre-pregnancy counselling and she was utterly amazing and we talked for a bit. It turned out that I was allergic to Stemetil as well and developed a skin rash because of it. They tested my ketones which were 4+ at that point and immediately admitted me because I had lost 6kg which was more than 5% of my weight. I also had muscle atrophy which meant my muscles were wasting away and every part of my body hurt.

I started to feel better, but eating and drinking was still impossible

I stayed in hospital for a week, getting 8L of fluids while giving me IV Ondansetron and a high dose of Thiamine. I started to feel better, but eating and drinking was still impossible. Every bite would make me sick. Every sip would make me nauseous.

I was discharged when my ketones were slightly better and I was able to swallow tablets. The truth is, I shouldn't have left but I wanted to. During my stay there, I had developed a phobia for getting my blood pressure / heart rate checked. Every time I would hear them coming, my heart already started to race uncontrollably. One day, during my admission, they were taking my observations and I could feel it happening and so my heart rate went up to 150. They weren't sympathetic. They were panicking, and so I panicked even harder. I had another ECG done and even though my consultant was understanding and said it was anxiety, the nurses weren't. I ended up in a spiral of panicking as soon as that cuff was placed around me and just wanted to go home.

I closed my eyes because I just wanted it all to stop.

I had to go to the antenatal clinic every two weeks to be weighed as I kept losing weight until I was 15 weeks pregnant, they would check my blood pressure and review my medication. They gave me the maximum dose of

Ondansetron (a cancer medication) which I needed to take in combination with Metoclopramide, Thiamine, Folic Acid and Fortisip shakes.

My 12 week scan came up and I was absolutely dreading it. I hated the 40-minute taxi ride to hospital where it took everything from me to not be sick. I hated the waiting because I could barely sit up straight. I hated seeing everyone sitting there pregnant and smiling when all I wanted was to not be pregnant. I just wanted to crawl back in bed because I was so sick. Luckily, the Sonographer was very understanding and helpful. She offered to stop if I would feel sick and held my hand throughout. I didn't look at the screen because I was too sick. I closed my eyes because I just wanted it all to stop.

I had a check-up with my GP the day after and completely broke down. I couldn't stop crying. I explained to her that I wasn't excited about the pregnancy and that I didn't want to wake up anymore. She was very gentle, but offered no real solution. She wanted me to start medication but because I was already on so many she wasn't sure which one she could give me. I waited until I had my appointment at the hospital again and explained what was going on. They did a mental health referral and started me on propranolol, a beta-blocker that takes away the physical symptoms. I was offered 10 CBT sessions and I was diagnosed with an anxiety- and panic disorder which I am currently still suffering from (I hate to use the word "suffering" because it's a part of me I have grown to love).

Every part that made me, me had disappeared

My second trimester was relatively quiet although the nausea never subsided and I wasn't able to eat anything substantial. I don't know how me, or my baby, survived when all I could eat was nuts and melon. I was signed off sick from work ever since I was pregnant but returned part-time (working from home) just before lockdown when I was around 20 weeks pregnant but it was really hard. I was tired all the time and even my consultant often told me that there's no shame in being signed off my entire pregnancy because I was just too sick. For me it was important to try and go back to work because I love work and I had already lost everything I loved. I'm a writer but I would vomit every time I looked at a screen. I loved reading but that would make me dizzy. Every part that made me, *me* had disappeared and I often wondered if this was really all worth it. It felt very isolated as well because me and my wife lived in London and our family lived in Belgium. It made things difficult because there was no one really checking in even though I don't think anyone really understood how serious it actually was.

The third trimester was quite rough again. The sickness came back, together with heartburn, and by the time I was 35 weeks pregnant I ended up in hospital again because my heart rate and blood pressure were far too high, there was sign of an infection and I felt very dizzy. When I was 36 week pregnant, the same thing happened again and they advised me to stop taking the Ondansetron because I was on it for so long now. I stopped taking it and the episodes went away. That did mean I wasn't taking anything for my sickness anymore which made the last few weeks quite unbearable. I went for my midwife appointment when I was 38 weeks pregnant and they immediately booked me in for an emergency scan the day after because I was measuring far too small. Luckily, our baby was still thriving. I, however, wasn't.

I gave birth when I was 39 weeks pregnant and even that was almost as traumatic as my pregnancy having to have lots of interventions (breaking my waters, putting me on a hormone drip, developing an infection during labour) and I sustained a third degree tear for which I needed to have surgery straight after. A lot of women describe the relief they feel after giving birth but I never felt that. I was extremely happy it was over but to feel this sick for nine months straight would leave an everlasting impact.

HOW I SURVIVED HYPEREMESIS GRAVIDARUM

Five weeks in and the sickness began,
Understand how I felt, nobody can.
Crazy thoughts rushed, I needed a break.
Unsure how much more my body could take.
What I'd been through was hard to believe,
Confused as to why I continued to breathe.
The constant sickness wouldn't leave me alone,
Trapped in my brain and a place I called home.
At my 12 week scan, the excitement had gone,
I closed my eyes, I couldn't bare to go on.
Emotionally drained, of course I would cry.
Physically exhausted, I wanted to die.
Diagnosed with a panic disorder and Anxiety,
I was offered 10 sessions of CBT.
How could growing a baby cause me so much pain,
Emotional stress and mental strain,
I finally gave birth, I was physically in tact,
But left with Invisible scars that would have a lasting impact.

- Stefanie

There was nothing I could do or say,
To take my wife's pain away.
To have to watch, broke my heart,
Why did this sickness have to start.
I made her food and cleaned the house,
After all, I am her spouse.
Those were the only things I could do,
To show I was there, I hope she knew.
I had to be strong, I had no choice,
I couldn't cry or raise my voice.
Hide what I feeling emotionally,
Even though this did drain me.
My feelings were always torn,
Happy at times but mentally worn.
The end of the pregnancy didn't seem near,
Many days I just wanted him here.
Excited to have a son to share,
I wanted it over, to end my wife's nightmare.

- Steffi B. (Stefanie's wife)

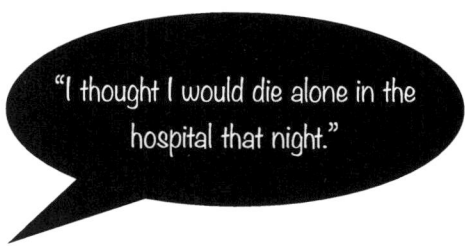

THE HG STORY OF... SARAH

In 2015 I found out I was pregnant with my first child and I was really excited. I had wanted to be a mum for so long. I had always imagined a perfect pregnancy where I would glow and enjoy every moment and have a perfect bump. My reality was unfortunately very different to my expectations.

I started to be sick first thing in the morning when I was around six weeks pregnant. As this was my first child and I had heard that sickness was normal during pregnancy, I was not concerned. As the days went by, my sickness window grew. I wasn't just sick in the mornings, I was sick in the afternoons and the evenings. I was bringing up most of the food I was eating and most fluids that I drank. This went on for about a week and I decided to tell my midwife as I did not know anyone else who was as sick, during their pregnancy as I was. The midwife was not concerned and told me she would check the ketones in my urine at my first appointment and if they were 4+ it would mean my body was dehydrated and I would go into hospital for fluids.

I attended my first appointment and my ketones were fine. I was really confused as to why my ketones were fine as I felt really poorly and hadn't eaten or drank properly for nearly two weeks. I continued to not be able to eat and drink for around four weeks, not reaching out for help, as I didn't know what help to reach out for and I was so weak. I would crawl into the bathroom and sit on the floor for a while crying in between dry heaving and I would only lift my head off the pillow to spit out my saliva.

My mum and my partner held both of my arms, one on each side and walked me to the doctors surgery

I was roughly 13 weeks pregnant when I saw my midwife

again. I struggled to get out of bed to even attend the appointment but my mum and my partner held both of my arms, one on each side and walked me to the doctors surgery. I had to stop after a few steps to retch and I would step and then retch, step and retch, it was horrendous. I was sick during the appointment and spitting into a cup as I couldn't control my saliva and I certainly couldn't swallow it. The midwife was not concerned about my spitting at the time and didn't understand why I was spitting and told me that I should just swallow it - I later found out that this was known as Hypersalivation and is a symptom of HG. My ketones were 4+ so the midwife rang the early pregnancy unit at my local hospital and explained that she was sending me in as an 'emergency'.

I got there after having to travel on two buses and having to wait nearly three hours to be seen. I was dry heaving lots in the waiting room and felt extremely weak. Thankfully I had my partner with me, so I was able to rest my head on him. I was finally called in to have my urine checked again, even though it had already been checked before at my midwife appointment. I could not wee, as I wasn't able to drink. The midwife told me to sit in the waiting room and try to drink as much as I could, until I was able to wee. My partner had to go to work, as we had been waiting for nearly five hours by this point. My mum came and took over to sit with me. I was sipping on bits of water and then instantly being sick with the water I had just sipped. I was able to squeeze a dribble of wee out eventually and they tested it and my ketones were apparently fine. They told me I needed to go home, I was too weak to care and argue. I couldn't believe I had sat in hospital all day, struggling to stay awake and heaving and being sick in front of many strangers to be told I had to go home and would not be getting any help. My mum was extremely cross and demanded that I be taken seriously and receive some care.

Made to feel like a burden

The midwife decided I could stay in for some fluids but made it clear that it was only because of the colour of my urine, that I was being allowed to stay in. My urine looked like muddy water. I was made to feel really unwanted and that I was wasting valuable time. The midwife said she would put my drip on fast so that the bed could be used for someone else.

I had blood taken earlier on in the day but had not yet received any results. As I was getting ready to leave, around five doctors came round my bed and closed the curtain and asked my mum where we were going. My mum explained that my drip was finished, so we were going home. The doctor said that I would not be going anywhere, as he had checked my blood result and my potassium salts were extremely low, so I needed to stay in hospital and be put onto a potassium drip. I had to say goodbye to my mum and go to a ward. I stayed on the ward for five days and my parents, sister and my partner came to visit me most days when they could.

I felt much better in the hospital and by the time I was discharged, I was able to eat and drink and I was given Metoclopramide, an anti-sickness medication to take home and a diagnosis of Hyperemesis Gravidarum. I had never heard of this condition and neither had any of my friends or family.

I was around 14 weeks pregnant now and was able to eat and drink a lot more. I would heave and be sick every morning and I stayed up past a certain time in the evenings but I felt better and had the energy to sit on the sofa, rather than lay in bed. I attended another midwife appointment around 16 weeks and unfortunately my sickness was deteriorating again.

The midwife said to call my GP, so I told my doctor and they suggested changing my sickness medication. I was then put on Cyclizine and that helped me for a few weeks but after a period of time, I would continue to be sick again, so I had to go back to my doctors and they would try another anti-sickness. The next one was Ondansetron. I had to take anti-sickness medication until the end of my pregnancy from around 13 weeks when it was finally issued to me. I was also told I needed to take folic acid and Vitamin C supplements, some days they stayed down, other days they did not.

The birth of Lihanna-Marie

I was sick at least once a day until I gave birth and I lost around three stone. I did not have much of a bump, which really made me sad, as I had hoped to have a maternity photoshoot. I did not enjoy being pregnant at all. Towards the end I felt a bit better but I wouldn't say any of it was enjoyable and I couldn't wait to give birth so that it would all be over. There were many days when I wanted my life to end and I resented my unborn baby for making me feel so poorly. I was at times debating an abortion, as I didn't feel that I would be able to go through a whole pregnancy being as poorly as I was.

I gave birth on the 16th of February 2016 to my first born daughter and we called her Lihanna-Marie Roberts. I fell in love instantly and all the horrible HG symptoms disappeared, being so poorly felt like a distant memory and I was so happy that I made it through!

Four amazing years had passed and I spoke to my partner about having another child, we were obviously worried because of how poorly I'd been with my first but I wasn't aware that the condition would come back. I was also told that every pregnancy was different. So we were hopeful that I would be okay and hopefully have a good second pregnancy. We were very wrong. I found out I was pregnant in February 2020 and we were at first, extremely happy. I contacted the doctors to get a midwife appointment and made it very clear about how much I had suffered with HG in my first pregnancy and I had hoped that I may have been monitored throughout my second pregnancy. I felt fine for about three weeks and I was so happy, I really felt like this pregnancy would be different and that I would not suffer.

HG came back even worse the second time

Unfortunately before I had even managed to have my first midwife appointment, the sickness started and it didn't just start with morning sickness like my first. It hit me hard from the moment it began. I was sick after eating a meal one day and from then on, I couldn't eat or drink hardly anything at all. I had also started to suffer early with Hypersalivation, so once again I found myself spitting into a cup that I carried around with me.

I went to my first midwife appointment and I was being sick during the appointment and my ketones were 4+ so I was sent to the hospital and my mum came with me. I remember thinking this was a good sign, I felt like they would help me sooner and that I would then be fine for the rest of my pregnancy, but unfortunately that was not the case. I went to the hospital and remember sipping on Ribena as I knew I would need to wee at the hospital, so I was trying to make sure I could. My ketones were still 4+ and they decided to give me a drip and I was really happy, as I felt like I was being treated with more respect and wasn't made to feel like I was wasting time. I had the drip and was able to go home. I was sent home with Cyclizine but was still sick everyday, although not as bad and I remember thinking to myself that I would now be able to cope with the small amount of sickness and enjoy the rest of my pregnancy.

The pandemic hit

COVID-19 came to the UK and everyone had to go into lockdown when I was around eight weeks pregnant. My sickness had started to get really bad again despite being on three Cyclizine tablets. I rang my midwife and GP but no professional would see me because of the virus. I was told that all of my future midwife appointments would be over the phone. No one could see how poorly I was, as no friends or family were allowed to come round to our house.

I couldn't even lift my head off my pillow

I just laid in bed feeling like I was going to die, as no one would help me. I once again found myself on the bathroom floor crying and telling my partner that I couldn't do it. I wanted my life to end, I had extreme thoughts of suicide but was too weak to actually attempt. My 4-year old would come and speak to me in my bedroom and my partner would tell her to leave me to rest, I couldn't even lift my head off my pillow to talk to her some days.

I was around 12 weeks pregnant and was still unable to eat or drink much at all. I attended my first scan, which I had to attend alone due to the virus and I was extremely weak. I was standing at the reception desk and my knees gave way, the receptionist got me a wheelchair and wheeled me to my scan. I remember crying to the midwife saying that I couldn't do it and I wanted to have an abortion. Of course that wasn't what I truly wanted but I couldn't imagine suffering again for the duration of this second pregnancy.

I felt defeated

I thought the drip in the hospital a few weeks before would have helped me but it didn't and the anti-sickness medication wasn't helping either and I couldn't find the strength to continue. The midwife checked my ketones and said they were fine. I explained that I'd not ate or drank properly in weeks and she said my body must be coping as my ketones were okay. Feeling defeated, I went back home and laid in bed for roughly six more weeks.

I tried to call my midwife and the early pregnancy unit to explain how bad the sickness was but all I was given were tips on what to eat and told to try ginger and suck on ice cubes. Basically all tips that work for morning sickness but this wasn't just morning sickness, this was Hyperemesis Gravidarum, which was completely different.

I begged them to help me and they said I could go to the early pregnancy unit but if my ketones were ok they would send me home, they were also saying that due to the virus they were reluctant to keep anyone in on a fluid drip. I was so weak and had very little energy, I was worried I'd have to travel all the way to the hospital on my own to be turned away.

I eventually got the point where I stopped calling. I had given up. I wanted to die, I felt like I was dying. I just laid in bed and did not know if the next morning I would wake up. My 4-year old was watching her Mummy slowly deteriorate before her eyes and she didn't understand. My fiancé was losing his partner and I just wanted the pregnancy and my life to end.

There was no morning, afternoons or nights, all my days merged into one. I felt like I was just existing, not living. I was struggling to sleep, so a doctor prescribed me Promethazine over the phone, to help me to sleep and also to see if it would help my sickness. It did neither.

I had not seen my parents in roughly 10 weeks, we had spoken on the phone briefly due to the little energy I had, but due to lockdown we had not physically seen each other. They popped to my house to see me on the doorstep as they were growing concerned and wanted to see how I was. They were not happy with the way I looked, they could visibly see my weight loss and deterioration and forced me to call the hospital one last time.

My partner had tried previously to get me to call on many occasions but I refused and as he lived with me, he did not see the deterioration as dramatically as my parents did as they had not seen me for so long. I was upset as I didn't want to waste what little energy I had calling the hospital to be told that there was nothing that could be done and they wouldn't help me.

I rang and explained how long it had been since I had eaten a proper meal and I told them I had lost nearly four stone and said that I couldn't drink and told them how weak I was. They said I could go into the early pregnancy unit to be checked. I had to go in alone. My ketones were again fine and they were going to send me home but I used my last bit of energy to beg for a fluid drip and I collapsed in tears on the floor. I don't remember exactly what I said as It was all a blur but they decided I could stay for a drip but that I wouldn't be admitted due to the virus. I would be given a fast fluid drip and be going home as soon as it had finished.

They did not want to keep people in unnecessarily and no one knew the effects the virus had on pregnancies and unborn babies. They took some bloods and I sat waiting for the drip to finish, alone due to restrictions at the hospital. A doctor came to see me and explained that I would have to stay in overnight as my liver was not functioning correctly and they wanted me to have a liver scan.

They also found that once again my potassium salts were extremely low. I now know that this is called Hypokalemia and is life threatening. At the time though, I did not realise how serious it was, I was taken to a bed and attached to a potassium salt drip. I was drifting in and out of sleep and I remember all of a sudden my curtain came flying shut and around four doctors were stood around my bed saying that I needed to be transferred to intensive care because the potassium drip was not working, my body was not absorbing the potassium and my potassium was dangerously low and this could stop my heart.

Close to death

They needed to put me onto a heart monitoring machine as they were not sure if I would wake up in the morning. I was terrified and alone. All I could do was call my parents and my partner and speak to them and my little girl and tell them that I loved them. I could hardly talk on the phone as I was crying, I didn't know if that was my final goodbye to my loved ones and I genuinely thought I might die alone in the hospital that night.

Thankfully my heart did not stop and my body started to absorb the potassium. I was on a potassium drip for 48 hours as well as a fluid drip. My arms were bruised and sore from all of the cannulas and blood tests. I was given Prochlorperazine in hospital via an Intravenous drip but had a really funny turn. I felt like I had been sedated and it made me sleep for roughly 24 hours. I asked to change anti-sickness medication, as it really didn't agree with me. I was then put onto an Ondansetron drip to see how I would go.

I was put under the nutrition team at the hospital as they were concerned about my weight loss and they gave me Fortisip milkshakes to help me start to take in some calories again and help me to put back on some weight. If I was unable to stomach the milkshakes they were going to consider tube feeding. I struggled for a day or so to drink them but thankfully I started to be able to drink the milkshakes and progressed onto gradually eating food again.

I had to go for a liver scan whilst in hospital and this came back to say that my liver was still not functioning as well as they had hoped. I was in hospital for a week, roughly and I didn't get to have any visitors due to the virus. I could not wait to go home. I was sent home with Ondansetron tablets and Potassium tablets. I was also assigned a consultant who I would meet with once a month and she would check my bloods to ensure my potassium was not falling again.

By the time I was 20 weeks, I was able to eat and drink a bit more and even had the energy to be able to sit on the sofa and talk to my daughter and partner. I was sick, heaving and nauseous every day still and would still have heartburn every morning. This continued throughout my whole pregnancy. I remember also having terrible constipation when I started to eat again, my body really struggled to deal with the fact I had food in my tummy as my digestive system had not needed to work for months.

The Birth of Layla-Mya

The day finally came where I gave birth to my second daughter, on the 16th of October 2020. We named her Layla-Mya Roberts. I remember crying and saying to my partner 'I did it' I was so proud and overwhelmed that I had made it through a second HG pregnancy. I would love to have more children but unfortunately I now know that HG tends to come back and gets worse with each pregnancy. So unfortunately I will not be having any more children as I can not risk losing my life and my two beautiful girls losing their Mummy. I am so grateful for the two daughters that I have been blessed with and I love them very much.

HOW I SURVIVED HYPEREMESIS GRAVIDARUM

I always imagined pregnancy to be bliss.
Why am I suffering, I didn't plan this.
The gagging, the nausea and constant sickness.
Had caused my body and mind incredible weakness.
Thoughts of abortion and resentment filled my head.
There were many times, I wished I was dead.
When expecting a baby, how could that be?
Pregnancy was unfortunately awful for me.
Months stuck in bed, a prisoner in my own home.
No one understood my condition, I felt so alone.
I had tried what felt like every medication.
Whilst dealing with awful side effects like hypersalivation
Nights and days merged, I was just existing.
I tried to get professional help, but no one was listening.
I kept being told you'll be fine, sickness is normal.
Confused as to why I was feeling so awful.
My first pregnancy was bad but I tried again.
Maybe a one off I thought. Wrong, it returned but times ten.
Both times around I was very close to death.
Before sleeping at night, had I taken my last breath?
Even though I suffered greatly with my first, I braved it once more.
I'm so proud I survived and have two girls to adore.

- Sarah Titmus

HOW I SURVIVED HYPEREMESIS GRAVIDARUM

It was so hard to sit and watch, my partner nearly die.
I'm a man so of course I thought, I must not let her see me cry.
I had to watch her become so weak,
At times she was unable to speak.
Her deterioration was surprisingly fast,
As the weeks and months went past.
I felt helpless, as she lay in bed,
She couldn't even lift her head.
The hospital at times would not help,
All I wanted to do was scream and yelp.
I didn't no most days if she would awaken,
I was on edge worrying about whether her life would be taken.
She was growing our baby, of course I could not wait.
But to see her suffer, filled my heart with hate.
I had to become both mum and dad for our eldest child,
Whilst worrying thoughts were zooming round my head, driving me wild.
I love this lady with all my heart,
I watched her suffer right from the start.
She was strong and made it through,
Not just once, she braved two.
- Haydn (Sarah's fiancé)

This too shall pass

"The worst nightmare of my life"

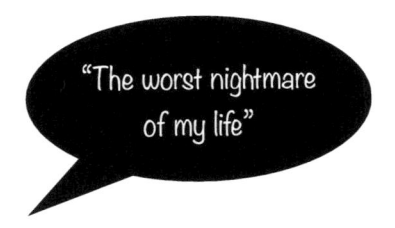

THE HG STORY OF...
ABBI

Ever since I can remember I've always wanted to be a mum. I would babysit for friends and hold babies every chance I got. I would always say: "I can't wait to get married and have kids of my own". Every pregnant woman I had seen looked happy, and healthy, and nine months later they would have their baby no questions asked. Little did I know the complications I would face to become a mum myself.

After my husband and I got married, we decided to wait a few years before having children which was hard as we were both desperate to start a family. After 4 1/2yrs of marriage, I fell pregnant and we were both so happy! We couldn't believe we were going to be parents. Sadly we lost our first child through miscarriage which was extremely upsetting for us both. We were so happy but felt apprehensive as well when I fell pregnant again. We were worried we would lose our second child too.

Fighting to get the right care

At five weeks, the nausea started. At first, I thought this was a positive sign. But then, the smell of coffee and cooking made me heave. Little did I know what was to come. I began to vomit in the morning and the nausea was just always there. I could hardly eat as I felt too sick. The thought of even trying to put food in my mouth made me gag. I went to the doctors and was prescribed some Cyclizine and was told to eat ginger biscuits to help with the nausea. The Cyclizine didn't work and only made me sleepy so I stopped using it.

At six weeks, the vomiting got worse. I was always nauseous and was vomiting 20-30 times a day all through the night. I went back to the doctor to get signed off work, and to ask for other medication as there was no way I could even drive or sit in front of a screen all day to do my job. The only advice I got was: eat some chocolate and go round your friends house to take your mind off it. That was the last thing I wanted to do! There was still no improvement 48 hours later so I went back to the doctors and saw someone else in hopes that I would get some helpful advice and better medication during my third visit. I was told to have fruit smoothies, ice lollies and ginger tea. No help with medication or anything. They said I had morning sickness and it would pass. All three doctors clearly had no idea how poorly I was. I was so angry, frustrated and annoyed. Surely I wasn't the only woman who could be this sick and be offered no help. All I could think of was that they were scared to prescribe anything that could harm my baby in case I tried to sue them for negligence.

Then, I remembered the Duchess of Cambridge being really sick with Hyperemesis Gravidarum (HG) and I looked into it. By this time, I couldn't eat or even hold water down. I was vomiting over 30-40 times a day. I couldn't even swallow my saliva so I had to constantly spit it in my sick bucket. My body was weak and tired. I ached all over from retching so much as my body had no fluids to get rid of. I was confined to my bedroom as any smell made me feel even worse. Any noise or light gave me headaches and I couldn't even look at my phone. I couldn't sleep as the nausea and vomiting was so bad and I was completely exhausted.

I couldn't believe what was happening to me. All my friends had said they didn't really feel sick and they all were able to carry on with their daily lives as normal. Why not me? Why am I so sick? I read up on HG and was sure I had it. What else could it be?

At 7 1/2 weeks, I went to the early pregnancy unit (EPU) as I had some cramping and wanted to be sure I wasn't miscarrying again. It took every bit of strength in my body just to drive the six miles to the hospital without vomiting and walking to the unit. My legs were so shaky I nearly collapsed as I had no strength after lying in bed for a few weeks. Thankfully, our baby was fine and I got to see a heartbeat! This was huge as it gave me a hope and a purpose for going through this horrendous sickness.

I begged the receptionist for help with my vomiting after explaining no doctor would help. I got referred to the Gynaecology Ambulatory Unit (GAMBU); a place specifically for those suffering with HG. After checking my hydration levels, they found I was severely dehydrated and my ketones were 4++ so they gave me an injection of Ondansetron, an anti-sickness drug, and my vomiting stopped for a few hours and the nausea faded. They gave me some more of the medication to take home to stop me being sick. I thought I would finally be ok and start feeling better as I was able to eat a little and felt slightly human again. I thought the hospital had finally found a cure for this awful sickness.

A never ending cycle of pregnancy sickness

By the next morning, the pills didn't work anymore and the vomiting began again as the injection had run its course. I waited 24 hours but nothing changed. I still couldn't eat or drink and would be vomited straight back out. The smell alone of even just some dry toast made me heave and gag. I went back to GAMBU and they put me on a drip of IV fluids and IV Ondansetron. The instant relief felt amazing. I was in hospital all day to get my fluid levels back up and went home that night feeling much better. I continued the Ondansetron pills at home hoping they would work this time. By midnight the vomiting started again and the pills hadn't worked for a second time so I went back to GAMBU for more IV fluids and medication. This continued on nearly a daily occurance with A&E trips at the weekend when GAMBU was closed just to try to keep me going with fluids and IV anti-sickness.

There was no way I could go back to work with how poorly I was. My sick note was about to run out so I needed to make a decision. There was no support from my manager, except constant emails and voicemails wanting to know when I would be returning to work as they had no cover for me even though I had provided them with sick notes. I tried to explain how sick I was but they didn't understand. I couldn't deal with the stress so my only option was to quit.

I was gutted and knew it would financially impact me but what choice did I have? The gynaecologist doctor said the symptoms would lessen around 15-20 weeks and so there was no way I could put in a 40-hour week at work anymore with the workload I would be given upon my return. I had been off for two months. Once I resigned, I felt relieved that I could concentrate on the health of me and my baby.

I was losing weight so fast and I could hardly walk because I was so weak. At nine weeks, I had lost 10kgs. I had been confined to my bedroom from week six and didn't have the energy to even climb the stairs. My husband had to stand outside the shower to make sure I didn't collapse as I had no strength in my legs to wash myself. I cried day and night wanting this sickness to go away. I couldn't do it anymore and the thought of carrying on like this for months made it even worse. I was counting down the hours and trying to sleep to forget about it. It honestly felt like the worst nightmare of my life that no one could wake me up from. Many times the thought of ending my pregnancy crossed my mind but I just couldn't do it as I had a little person growing inside me and it wasn't their fault I was so unwell.

I knew I had to do everything in my power to help this little person thrive and give them the best chance possible no matter how hard it was.

My husband was an absolute rock and was so supportive. Sadly, he worked all day so was out from 7am-8pm. I missed him and just wanted cuddles but the smell of his deodorant and aftershave made my nausea worse. My husband just wanted to help and support me but when he tried it made me feel worse. He felt so helpless.

At nine weeks, my symptoms hadn't improved at all and my constant trips to hospital were really taking their toll. The gynaecologist doctor decided to try Metoclopramide alongside the Ondansetron to see if it would help. Sadly it didn't and the vomiting and the daily trips to hospital continued.

At 12 weeks, I looked so skinny and weak. No baby bump to be seen. No one looking at me would even guess I was pregnant. None of my clothes fit anymore due to my weight loss. I looked pale and my arms and hands were covered in bruises from the many needles and cannulas for all the fluids and IV medications I was receiving. My veins had all collapsed within the first few weeks of pregnancy as I was so dehydrated. It took four or five tries each day before they could reach a vein so, finally, they left the cannulas in for several days to minimise any discomfort.

A referral to the home care team

The midwife in charge of GAMBU made the decision to refer me to the home care team and to look into further treatment for me to try to keep me out of hospital and to get the vomiting under control to stop losing weight. My only option, apart from being admitted, was steroids. They were given to me twice a day at home by a nurse along with the Ondansatron as well as Clexane injections to stop me from getting blood clots. This went on for 8 weeks until I was 20 weeks pregnant. The steroids stopped 95% of the vomiting and I could finally start to eat, however, due to months of vomiting, my stomach rejected what I was eating. I just remember crying. My body was so malnourished and I was so hungry that I felt like a complete and utter failure. It took a good week or two before this finally stopped and I could eat properly. It felt like a luxury and I had forgotten how good food tasted.

At 20 weeks, I came off the steroids and could finally start taking the Ondansatron and Metoclopramide tablets. I was still sick a few times especially if I forgot to take my medication but I finally felt better. I started to slowly build my strength and gain some weight. I was so happy to finally be out of hospital and be at home.

At 28 weeks, I was able to see my friends who I hadn't seen in seven months. I had worked really hard to build up the strength to get out of the house. I was able to get my hair done which felt amazing! I still hardly had a bump and you could pass it as bloating as I was still so small.

Due to me being a high risk pregnancy I was having scans every few weeks to check if our baby was growing well.

At our 37-week growth scan, the Sonographer looked confused. All I could see on the scan was 32/33. I asked him: baby hasn't grown? He said no. He referred me to the consultant and I asked if the baby would be delivered early. They said they would wait until 39 weeks. I was very annoyed and said why after all I'd been through my whole pregnancy would my baby just be left for 2 more weeks? I was so angry that I felt like my baby and I were put at risk by waiting. They agreed to do a stretch and sweep at 38 weeks and induce me at 39 week.

At my 38-week stretch and sweep, they noticed some protein in my urine and my blood pressure was slightly raised. They sent the urine off to check it. That night they called me to go in the next day to get checked as they were concerned because of the level of protein in my urine. I was beside myself with worry after getting this call. Suddenly, I had the worst exploding headache ever come on like I'd never had before. I first thought it was just stress but then I also had the worst pain under my rib cage like someone had kicked me in the stomach and was tightening a belt round me. I knew then something wasn't right. I called the labour ward and they admitted me straight away.

The final stretch

After some quick checks, they confirmed I had pre-eclampsia and induced me. My blood pressure was sky high and I had 4++ of protein in my urine. They said I had been a ticking time bomb for weeks which is part of the reason my baby had stopped growing but it didn't show on the scans. I was completely exhausted and couldn't believe there was another complication to consider. I was given some medication to help bring my blood pressure down and they put me on a drip.

My labour was very quick and intense with back to back contractions that not even an epidural could prevent the excruciating pain I was in. I was still sick from the HG and just wanted it all to end. I just wanted my baby out and safe but the baby's heartbeat dropped very low so the emergency buzzer was pulled and a load of doctors came in to quickly get the baby out. Thankfully my baby was fine and safely delivered within minutes.

I was in shock. This tiny human I had waited so long for

was here safe in my arms. Completely perfect in every way. All the sickness, complications, and worry were over. Finally I could breathe a sigh of relief.

Was it worth it? Absolutely! Would I do it again? Yes definitely. The thought of it petrifies me but now I know what to expect. I won't take no for an answer and I know how to get the help I need so I don't suffer so much.

Each day I show myself my deep inner strength

> "The sicker the mum, the better for the baby"

THE HG STORY OF... KATE

I am Kate Daems, a 31-year old kindergarten teacher living in Belgium.

Grade 3 human papillomavirus

My HG journey started when I was 28 year old and diagnosed with grade 3 human papillomavirus which meant I had a higher risk of developing cervical cancer. Luckily, I got treated on time and was told I would have no trouble conceiving. However, there was the risk of having to go through another procedure which meant my cervix would become too short to continue the pregnancy but after talking things through with my husband we decided to try for a baby after all.

I made an appointment with the doctor in September 2019 after I had just turned 30. After a few blood tests, I decided to stop taking the pill in October. I wanted to get the medication out of my system first so we decided not to have sex during the fertile days and as little as possible in October / November. I was completely shocked when I found out in December that I was pregnant!

On 23 December, I went to the doctor for a blood test which is standard in Belgium. He confirmed that I was already eight weeks pregnant by then.

The sicker the mum, the better for the baby

Everyone started to ask me if I was feeling sick already, but I felt quite good... until Christmas Eve. I wasn't hungry at all and when I woke up the next day, the illness only got worse.... My scent became so strong that the slightest smells made me incredibly nauseous. My husband made fresh meat buns, awful! He didn't understand me at all at the beginning!

When I was ten weeks pregnant, I went to the gynaecologist and told her I was sick but she told me that this was to be expected. She even said: "the sicker the mom, the better for the baby!' Only, everything got worse after that ...

Because I was not allowed to go to work anymore, I felt very lonely. In Belgium you immediately have to stop working if you're a kindergarten teacher and pregnant. I slept from 9PM to 10AM, then was awake for an hour and went back to sleep before 5PM. When I slept, I felt good and didn't feel the nausea. I was so tired. I couldn't do anything in the house. I just felt so weak. I vomited every time I lifted my head. It hurt my esophagus so much after a while.

After two weeks, I had already lost 6 kilos because I just couldn't eat. I called my mom to say that I could not bear this anymore, I could not even keep water in. Plus, there

was also the horrible excessive saliva. We drove together to the doctor where I got Primperan (Metoclopramide).
It allowed me to keep some water in, but it completely drugged me.

At 12 weeks pregnant I had to go back to my gynaecologist. When I told her, I had already lost 10kg, she got angry and said I should have come back when the previous consultant said it was actually a good thing to be this sick. They tested my ketones but they were fine so I wasn't admitted to hospital.

I felt horrible because this sickness wouldn't end. Everyone said it would get better after 12 weeks, but it didn't. I was so focused on getting to 12 weeks but it didn't change anything. I cried so much.

When I was 20 weeks pregnant, I almost passed out during the ultrasound. This was at the height of the corona pandemic on the 2nd of April. I was all alone at the gynaecologist without any support which I really needed.

The birth of Lenne

I finally started to feel better from 20 weeks onwards. I had to be careful not to pass out though and lay on my left side because it made me feel better.

Fortunately, I was able to enjoy the time I had left with my little baby in my tummy even though I never felt great. I kept having a bad taste in my mouth, and, even though the nausea subsided, and the salivation decreased, it was always there, lurking.

The last couple of weeks of pregnancy, the nausea returned because there was so much movement. But then our beautiful daughter Lenne was born on 24 August, 2020.

The best day of my life!

I lovingly accept all my feelings

"Lost over 10% of my body weight."

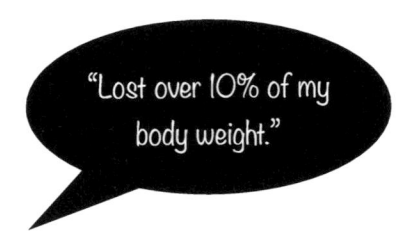

THE HG STORY OF... SIERRA

I didn't get diagnosed with HG until I was around 14 weeks pregnant. Prior to this I tried every combination of medication that the doctors were willing to give me, during the first trimester and into the beginning of my second trimester. I struggled the whole time! I had tried to get professionals to listen to me. I told them that something wasn't right and that I couldn't keep anything down, including drinks. I worked night shifts in the hospital during the COVID-19 pandemic, which added to my body's strain. There was nothing that I could do that would work and I felt as if no one was listening to me. The first time they sent me in to hospital for fluids, I was 12 weeks pregnant and had lost 15lbs, which was over 10% of my body weight! I had another visit to the emergency room, due to being so dehydrated that my vision was going blurry. I felt lightheaded and dizzy even when I was sitting down. The midwife at the hospital admitted me, but sent me home the next day and dismissed all of my concerns. Even though I still couldn't eat or drink and I was puking up stomach acid because I had nothing left in my system.

My HG did not matter

My doctor came up with a plan to put in a PICC line, have a Zofran (Ondansetron) pump and have intravenous fluids running. Another doctor from his office told me she would only be putting the PICC line in because my doctor told her the other treatment had to be ordered. She told me that my HG wasn't severe and I felt as if my HG didn't count. By this point, I had lost 21lbs, lost all of my muscle tone and colour! I had never felt so belittled in my life. It was as if, what I was feeling and dealing with was not valid. If I wasn't puking, I would be dry heaving and my nausea level was well passed level ten. I had to stop working because I couldn't function or move. The PICC line with fluids and Zofran (Ondansetron) had prevented me from vomiting and definitely lessened the dry heaving, but I still struggled with nausea every single day.

Taking each day as it comes

I am currently still pregnant, some days are better than others, but better, doesn't mean that I feel great and can do whatever I want. A good day might mean that my nausea is like a four or a five and I might be able to go to the store. Definitely not for long and after I get back home I can't do anything else that day. I never thought a pregnancy could be so rough, where you can't enjoy much at all. I still can't work, even at 25 weeks because I still need everything through my PICC line and have little energy most days. I have also never been one to be depressed, but when my whole life is put on hold that is really all I can feel. I feel like a burden most days on my family, financially and physically. I wouldn't trade my baby for anything and can't wait until she is born. I just hate that HG takes away the enjoyment from my pregnancy.

Learning to cope

The best way I have learned to cope with HG is finding people who understand all my thoughts and feelings without judgment! This experience so far has taught me how much you have to advocate for yourself, no matter your age or degree you carry. I've done my own research and can't believe how many people don't know anything about HG and that includes the professionals treating it. My hope is that one day this condition will be well known and women know there is a community that can help.

I can do this. I am doing this.

> "I couldn't have this baby."

THE HG STORY OF...
ANONYMOUS

HG where do I start… HG is the worst thing I have ever experienced in my life. It broke me and my partner; physically, mentally and emotionally. I thought I was a strong person until I met HG. I remember being excited for the first few weeks, after finding out we were expecting our first baby. Despite not being together very long, we both wanted to be parents. I purchased the announcement cards for the family and we looked at baby names. I am glad I had experienced this happy time, but also wish I could have been preparing for what was to come.

It didn't take long for the sickness to completely take over It started with slight sickness and nausea at six weeks, gradually building up to all day sickness and constant nausea. Within a week I was stuck in bed with debilitating nausea. In that week, I saw two doctors, one was at my own surgery and one was an emergency out of hours GP. I wasn't keeping any food or water down and I was losing weight rapidly. Both doctors told me it was normal morning sickness and that I just had to get on with it. I believed them. I remember thinking, It must be me, there must be something wrong with me and maybe it was all in my head. I carried on being bed bound and losing weight, I was eating very little to nothing most days. By the time I had my eight week midwife appointment, I had lost over a stone in weight and weighed just over 7 stone. I still don't know how I made it to that midwife appointment. I was so weak, I leant on my partner from the car, all the way to the doctor's office.

Finally someone listened

After doing a urine sample (what little I could provide) and being sick several times, my midwife sent me straight to A&E and rang the hospital. My midwife told me that my body was in ketosis and was eating away at my fat and muscle to keep me alive. I stayed at the hospital overnight and had four bags of fluid and anti-sickness. They bought me the worst fish and chips for tea but to me they tasted amazing, as it was the first food I had been able to eat in weeks and I was actually enjoying eating it. I made my partner go home and make me loads of food and sandwiches so I could sit and eat it all in the hospital. The next day I was discharged with Ondansetron and felt so much better. I even had an appetite, the nausea was still there but this was manageable. We went food shopping on the way home and I put EVERYTHING in the trolley, little did I know none of it would get eaten.

The sickness was back

The next day I woke up and it hit me all over again, I could smell everything; I could smell the rain outside, the kitchen cupboards, the new carpet downstairs, the washing powder on the bedding. I could barely open my eyes, daylight, even with curtains closed was far too bright and triggered the sickness. Any movement also triggered sickness.

The next few days I didn't move unless it was to be sat next to the toilet. Over the next month or so I tried various medications, some I could keep down, some I couldn't. The doctors tried me on everything and nothing I tried, really worked. I could just about cope with the sickness, because I got a few minutes of relief before the nausea would kick in again, but the nausea was debilitating. Most days I couldn't even wash or go downstairs. I couldn't even move rooms because the change in smell would trigger my nausea. The acid from my stomach was taking the enamel off my teeth, so I was advised to keep brushing to a minimum. This was actually a blessing, as I struggled with anything in my mouth.

I probably managed to brush my hair once a week, after my partner had washed it for me in the bath, as I was too weak most days to shower. I remember everyone else being so excited and I wasn't in the slightest bit excited, I was hating every minute of being pregnant. When I was around ten weeks pregnant, I sobbed for hours one night. I had reached breaking point, I told my partner I couldn't do it anymore and I didn't want the baby, as I couldn't do another 30 weeks of the daily hell I was in.

The mental struggles impacted our relationship

This was my life for four to five months. I would count down the 12 hours during the day for my partner to come home, just so I would have an hour of company. By 12 weeks it was really starting to affect me mentally, I was very isolated and lonely and I was anxious about the silliest of things. I would overthink and over analyse everything. My partner didn't often go out, other than to go to work, but when he did go out, I resented him as I hated being alone. We started to grow apart, he spent more nights going out leaving me alone and we started to hate each. I guess I partly blamed him for the way I was feeling and he hated me because this wasn't what we imagined, plus he couldn't do anything to help me. We both missed the people we were pre-pregnancy; fun, outgoing, hardworking, career driven, busy people. I was a shadow of the person I was and my partner was spending more time with his friends and going out drinking. I guess this was his way of coping.

The sickness and nausea started to become manageable by around 20 weeks. However, not long after starting to manage, I was referred for a perinatal mental assessment and diagnosed with perinatal anxiety. I was offered medication but I didn't want to take it on top of the medication I was already taking for the sickness. I struggled with being at home alone, as I had recently moved 60 miles away from all my friends and family. For months, most days, I only saw my partner for an hour or so and that was it.

By the time I was 28 weeks we were both really struggling as a couple, we argued constantly. I didn't understand him and he didn't understand me and we hated each other and I decided to move back home to live with my Dad. I moved all my midwifery and NHS care over and registered for birth at a different hospital. The next ten weeks we didn't really see each other and would go weeks without talking to each other. I attended all of my appointments alone and I was mentally preparing for becoming a single mum.

The Birth

The birth was amazing , I would have given birth to Jack ten times over, rather than go through the pregnancy. My partner was also amazing. Over the first six months of Jack's life we worked really hard to be good parents, even though we were living 60 miles apart. After six months of couples therapy and a lot of hard work, we all moved back in together. Things were amazing and we actually liked each other again, HG didn't break us. I knew then that I would never have another baby, as I couldn't go through that hell again. I knew Jack would be my only child but I was happy with that.

I couldn't have this baby

Then when Jack was 11 months old, despite birth control and breastfeeding, I found out I was pregnant. I would say the following few weeks were the second worst weeks of my life and I'm holding back the tears writing about my experience. I knew I could not have this child, there was an 80% chance of having HG again. No matter how much I didn't want the other option, there was no way I could be SO poorly and look after a one year old. Our relationship wouldn't make it through another HG pregnancy. We had only just recovered from the last one and I knew our little boy deserved better than what would be on offer if we went ahead with the pregnancy. Not many people know about this for fear of judgement. The 2nd of January 2019 was the worst day of my life. HG made the decision for me. Despite having a termination, it was very much felt as a loss. I left the clinic and broke down in tears, holding onto my partner saying "I just killed my own baby, what kind of a mum does that make me?" I got on with my life, the year was hard but I put on a good front. I felt like I didn't deserve to feel grief because I had caused it. I cried a lot when I was alone on my drive to work, it would always get me. I would wonder if it was a boy or a girl and who they might have been. It's something that sticks with me forever.

I made preparations for a second child

Three years later I started to feel guilty that I was depriving

Jack of a sibling and I wondered if maybe I could go through it again. If I took medication early enough I might be ok. After a few months of overthinking and working up the courage, I decided to get in touch with Pregnancy Sickness Support who sent me a preparation pack for HG. It had names of specialist consultants and hospitals in the UK who specialise in HG. They also put me in touch with a peer supporter who would support me through a HG pregnancy and be my voice or offer support and advice if and when needed. I got in touch with my doctor and after a few forceful conversations, he referred me to one of the consultants. I had also done a lot of research online and was in every forum and every support page.

I had heard of a new medication called Xonvea that only came to the UK in 2018, people in the USA and Canada say amazing things about it. I requested to try this medication and my doctor told me he had never heard of it, but the consultant had and said they would try me on It. It was a private prescription (£38 for 20 tablets!) She advised me to start taking it as soon as I had a positive pregnancy test and registered me with the local hospital so that I could go for IV Fluid drop in sessions whenever I felt I needed it. So I got brave – my partner and I made a childcare plan and prepared in every way possible for me to be bed bound for the next six months.

I was brave

Getting a positive pregnancy test this time was very different, I had feelings of happiness and fear at the same time, almost a feeling of regret as soon as it happened. I had my medication ready and I spoke to my boss at work. I told her the chances are high, that I am going to be off work for a long time once the sickness kicks in. I was hopeful the medication would prevent me from hospitalisation and would let me at least keep fluids down but I didn't expect miracles. I mentally prepared myself for Hell round two. I emotionally read every bedtime story with Jack for the next two weeks knowing I soon would not be able to. I cried because I already felt bad for not being the mum he deserved before I was even sick. I was petrified waiting for it to kick in and at six weeks it did. I had forgotten just how awful it felt. The sickness I could cope with but the nausea was unbearable it brought back so many memories and feelings and the first thing I thought was 'what have I done?'

That night I upped my medication to three tablets a day. The next day I felt almost fine… it was literally a miracle. The next ten weeks I would say I suffered with 'normal morning/all day sickness.' I am now 16 weeks pregnant and I am actually enjoying my pregnancy. I have the usual food aversions and sickness most mornings. I have bad days but they are nothing compared to how I suffered with HG. I have put weight on and managed to eat every day! I am so grateful to be pregnant and to have medication that is working for me. I am grateful for Pregnancy Sickness Support and for my peer supporter, who checks in with me to make sure that I'm ok. I am also grateful for the specialist consultant and for my partner for telling me I'm doing an amazing job every day. Most of all I'm grateful that I am still able to be a mum to my little boy!

I honour my baby and my body

"I felt like a failure."

THE HG STORY OF...
CONSYLINE

I promised myself to share my story as soon as I got my strength back, only to keep postponing. I realised that I was postponing out of fear. Fear that it will bring back the pain that I wanted to forget.

A day after I missed my period, I took a pregnancy test in the morning, there were two pink lines getting clearer and clearer. I felt a burst of joy that poured out in the form of tears. That was the fourth week of my pregnancy. The fifth week into my pregnancy is when I felt sick, I couldn't eat and I would vomit up to 40 times a day. By week six things had gone pretty much downhill, I had not told anyone about my pregnancy yet. I started losing weight due to vomiting. Every time I would vomit, I strained my muscles and ripped the lining of my oesophagus. I did my best to control the nausea but I felt helpless. It felt like a mix of food poisoning, car sickness and a roller-coaster ride all in one. I went to the hospital because things had got serious and started to show in my blood tests.

Hospital admission

I was finally admitted into hospital. That was the first time when I was introduced to the term 'ketone level.' A term every woman who suffers from HG and severe morning sickness is very familiar with. My ketones were high, despite getting all nutrition through IV. The nausea stuck with me. Vomiting on an empty stomach took the pain to a whole new level, I was throwing up acid and there was a burning sensation on the inside. In the following few weeks, I lost 20 kgs, became very weak and was completely dependent. I felt useless and like a failure. I worried about my pregnancy and the health of my baby.

Light at the end of the tunnel

I want to remind everyone that this is not just my story, this is on behalf of all HG sufferers. If you know someone going through something similar, you have no idea how much your support can make a difference. There are a lot of women out there who have worse experiences with HG. Those amazing and strong women are true heroes. And anyone who is suffering from HG and reading my story, just hang in there, the pain, loneliness and the sleepless nights will soon become a memory and you will have a beautiful baby to make up for it all.

One of the few things that I have learnt and helped me understand HG is finding and joining HG support groups on Facebook and other social media. Also, reading articles about HG has helped me immensely and reading other ladies stories made me feel like I wasn't alone and it helped give me the boost I needed not to give up.

I am powerful and strong

> "I couldn't cope with it at all."

THE HG STORY OF... SARAH JANE WARNER

I am currently 20 weeks pregnant with my second child. I had HG with my first pregnancy and I swore I would never put myself through it again. However, the desire to give my daughter a sibling was so great that we decided to try again. My husband was working from home due to COVID-19 and so we thought it was the best time to try, as he would be around if I was poorly again. I hoped I wouldn't get HG again – but unfortunately I did.

I feel the key to anyone deciding to try again is to be prepared. I spoke to a counsellor and GP before getting pregnant to discuss my ideas and thankfully the GP was supportive and agreed to first line meds when I had a positive test result. I have still been very poorly during this pregnancy and I've also needed second line meds again. However, I did feel more prepared with the knowledge of what was to come, this made me worry a little less. It was still horrible to go through it again and I had many low moments and times when I once again said I couldn't cope with it all. By taking one day at a time and even some days one hour at a time, I somehow pushed on. My husband was very supportive and I think that makes a massive difference when responsibilities can be covered by someone else.

For me HG is relentless - weeks and months of struggling with daily sickness, nausea and hypersalivation. Three months off work with my first child and a sense of loneliness and frustration that people didn't really get how bad it was. I struggled to keep down water at times and in both pregnancies I was close to hospital admission, but somehow managed to get by without. I also had severe constipation linked to dehydration and tablet side effects that meant I had to use suppositories and mini enemas to try and help. I still have haemorrhoids as a result of this that are causing issues at the moment.

However at 20 weeks and on five tablets a day I have started to have no actual sickness, just nausea. So hopefully it will become less and less over time. I realise I am lucky that the medication is allowing me to feel a bit better than I did as there are women who experience HG so much worse than I do, and I have the utmost respect for people who are on this journey.

Getting the support I need

HG is not normal morning sickness. HG is not something that all women experience. It is totally unexpected and made me feel the most poorly I have ever felt in my life. Thankfully Pregnancy Sickness Support were on hand to support me all the way. They give information, support workers, forums to chat to others and so much more. They are a lifeline. I would greatly advise anyone suffering from HG to get in touch and get help… we are not meant to deal with our HG journey alone!

During my first pregnancy I took medication up until birth. I am hoping I will be able to drop the amount of medication this time, but only time will tell. The biggest thing to say is that as cliché as it sounds... the end goal is so beautiful and so special that it makes everything worth it. But by no means is it an easy thing to do. My thoughts are with anyone experiencing this. Keep pushing on... one hour at a time, get support around you and fight for your right to get support from key professionals, with Pregnancy Sickness Support to help you out along the way.

My mothering journey starts now

> "This is all my fault."

THE HG STORY OF...
KELLY

In early 2014, after 12 months of (im)patiently waiting for a much-desired positive pregnancy test, my husband and I decided that the following morning would be the day we would book to see our GP to discuss our fertility, the options available to us and start to piece our infertility puzzle together. An appointment was made for that afternoon but as we were getting ready for work, I had a sudden desire to take a pregnancy test and use up the last test in the pack…..it came back POSITIVE! I had expected my period the day before but I wasn't expecting this news at all! I stumbled downstairs shrieking at my husband, absolutely stunned. What were the chances of this happening today of all days! "I guess we won't be needing that GP appointment after all" he smiled.

Weeks ticked by, I felt different, like I was carrying the world inside me, but I was symptomless. Dr Google reminded me that I should be experiencing morning sickness, have sore breasts and feel exhausted… but I felt no different!? Sadly, this pregnancy ended at eight weeks and I was beside myself with grief. One day, through my tears, I uttered to my husband "I would've given anything to have been sick, anything to know that our baby was really there".

Fast forward a month or so later, a late period and another pregnancy test, I discovered that I was pregnant once again. My joy was hesitant and I prayed for those early pregnancy symptoms to arrive…

HG pregnancy after loss

Five or six weeks into my pregnancy, I was getting ready to leave my office job for the day and felt a wave of nausea wash over me out of absolutely nowhere. I just made it to the toilet in time when the sickness came. Could this be another pregnancy symptom at long last to join the list of sore breasts and tiredness?! "so much for it being called morning sickness eh" I said to my husband as we walked through our front door that evening.

The next day came and I was sick twice during the afternoon at work. The following day it increased. The day after that it came more frequently until it started to consume me and I could no longer function enough to go to work.

I open my eyes in the morning. Sick. Sit up. Sick. Walk to the bathroom. Sick. Wash my face. Sick. Back to bed. Sick. I open my mouth to answer my husband when he asks how I feel. Sick. My husband touches my foot in sympathy. Sick. The television goes on – it's the news. Sick. I turn over in bed. Sick. I briefly wonder if I'll ever eat again. Sick. Then sleep. Peace.

Days go by like this – sleeping, crying and being sick.

Surely this is not normal?

I love my baby and this is what I wanted!

I can't nourish myself, let alone nourish a baby who is relying on me.

Should I terminate my much-wanted pregnancy?

I miss my life.

I asked for this. This is all my fault.

I am having very dark thoughts and I can't cope like this.

After a week or so, my husband finally managed to get me in front of my GP, sick bowl in tow. Through my tears, I pleaded for help. I remember feeling so embarrassed - like I had bought all of this on myself. My urine was dipped and my concerned GP sent me straight to the hospital for IV fluids and anti-sickness treatment. The GP appointment began in despair, but it ended with a flood of relief that someone might be able to help me. Help and treatment was not something that had occurred to me in the midst of the sickness.

Hypere-something

At the hospital I received anti-sickness medication via injection, which instantly gave me some relief, then I was hooked up to IV fluids on a ward. I recall being told I had hypere-something but I don't remember ever feeling like the condition was fully explained to me or signposting given for further community support. I had a sinking feeling that just maybe no one really knew why my body had reacted so acutely to pregnancy. I was known on the ward as the 'hyperemesis lady' and I was the only one with the condition on a general medical ward. I felt isolated, confused and I missed home.

I left the hospital after five long days absolutely desperate to start feeling like I could enjoy my pregnancy and begin nourishing myself and my baby. I was terrified of being sick again despite responding well to the anti-sickness medication that I was taking daily. Although I wasn't often sick following this hospital stay, I experienced daily nausea until I was around 28 weeks pregnant when I tentatively began to scale back on the anti-sickness medication.

Hurrah – to my delight, I began feeling better. Despite desperately wanting the pregnancy, the whole experience was quite traumatic, and I spent a lot of time worrying about the state of my mental health, what HG may have done to my body and how it may have affected my unborn baby.

Becoming a midwife

Fast forward five years and my beautiful baby is no longer a baby, but a healthy, happy and oh so sassy child. Despite having a turbulent pregnancy, she is my shining light and the most wonderful gift. However, I am still frightened to be sick again. I rarely drink alcohol and I don't eat meat in a bid to reduce my chances of feeling or being sick. Amongst other things, suffering with HG led me to become a midwife myself and I began my training in 2020. I hope that my experiences will stand me in good stead when it comes to supporting pregnant people with HG during my career. I vow to never suggest that any HG sufferers try eating a ginger biscuit – brownie promise!

Love and deepest admiration to every HG sufferer and survivor out there. You are amazing and stronger than you'll ever know.

Every day is a step closer to meeting my baby

> "My life never returned to normal."

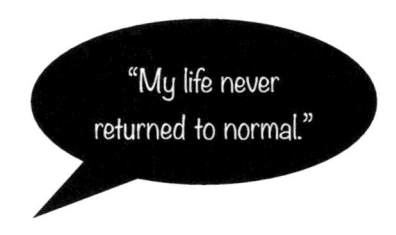

THE HG STORY OF...
DR DANIELLE

I'm one of the lucky ones, I was 24 years old when I moved to New Hampshire to start my new life as a wife. I had just finished touring as a professional figure skater and now had a wonderful job. This was with a small company in a small town in New Hampshire, while I coached skating part time. My days were busy from early in the morning to late at night. That was all about to change!

Due to touring with shows and moving many times, I missed the boat of being around a group of close friends who got married and had children around the same time. Not only did I not have anyone close to me who had gone through a pregnancy, my husband and I were both the youngest children in our families. Since neither of us babysat growing up, my expectations of pregnancy were therefore, from books and movies. Pop culture most commonly portrays pregnant women vomiting once or twice early on and then returning to normal life and also glowing. As you can guess, my life never returned to normal. I did not glow, I turned green.

I immediately started vomiting the day I missed my period and did not stop until I gave birth. Most of those nine months are now a blur, but I remember that I did my best to show up at work each day. It was the supportive women in my office who made me realise how dire my situation was, and that vomiting from morning through to the night was not normal, nor healthy.

In the United States, it is customary to have the first visit with an obstetrician around ten weeks into the pregnancy, so I had not yet seen my doctor. When I accepted the fact that I needed medical help, I called the doctor's office and was told to go to the hospital. My husband, who is in the US Marine Corps, was out of reach in Norway for military training, so I was on my own during this time. The hospital gave me bags of fluid and then discharged me. After my hospital visit, I was fortunate to have some friends take care of me until my husband returned home. They tried so hard to make me food that I could tolerate, yet nothing worked. Even crackers and ice pops would not stay in me. I suffered through the remaining months, taking it one day at a time. The only medication offered to me was Phenergan, (Promethazine) which made me sleep, and nutrition was never discussed. I don't even know if I was ever actually diagnosed with Hyperemesis Gravidarum (HG). It's truly a miracle that after nine months of malnourishment, I gave birth to a healthy baby girl.

Old Wives Tales

I had believed the old wives tales: "You're sick but the baby is getting all the necessary nutrients", "The sicker the better because it means you're having a strong pregnancy" and afterwards when I mentioned wanting more children, my doctor told me one of my favourites: "Just because it happened once, it might not happen again because each pregnancy is different." While this is true for some women, most HG mums have consecutive HG pregnancies.

Always optimistic and listening to my doctor, I went into my second pregnancy two and a half years later with the mindset that this time would be better, which proved to be a huge mistake. I had another nine months of barely being alive, only Phenergan (Promethazine) as a medication option and again nutrition was never discussed. My only memory of these nine months was being on my couch unable to sit up. I was lucky to have my step-daughter living with us because she helped with my toddler. The rest of that pregnancy is a fog. Again, I found out I was one of the lucky ones as I gave birth to another beautiful baby girl.

My third HG pregnancy

With my husband having dreams of a son, four years later, we decided to have a third child. I went into this pregnancy knowing full well that I would be dealing with HG. I was fortunate, as a US military spouse living on a small overseas military base. I had full medical coverage, a part-time nanny to help with my two young daughters, an underutilised hospital where I could get IV fluids and friends offering to help. I had a job I enjoyed as an administrator for our base WIC office (a nutrition program for pregnant mums and young children.) I had a co-worker who was a Registered Nurse, who was also an expert in nutrition and a devout patient advocate. I truly thought I had all my ducks in a row! Regardless of my positive thinking, I suffered another nightmare pregnancy. This one was full of medication mishaps; Reglan (Metoclopramide) gave me panic attacks, Phenergan (Promethazine) knocked me out and Zofran (Ondansetron) did not help. At least I had more options!

I received the same comments "You're pregnant so you should be sick" and "It happens to all of us" from friends, this time compiled with "You knew this would happen again, so we don't want to hear about it" from family. I was again fortunate to give birth to another healthy baby girl. My husband's dream of having a son would never be fulfilled. Although we are no longer married, to which HG played a direct role or potentially what caused my HG, our three daughters are our world. I can say that my 27 months of being malnourished and full of suffering, was worth it as I could not imagine my life without them.

Physical and Mental Health

HG took a toll on my physical and mental health, as it does with all HG sufferers. Due to HG, I was diagnosed with borderline gestational diabetes during my third pregnancy, with osteopenia decades before the average age of diagnosis. I had my first cavity after the first pregnancy and my marriage unfortunately did not survive. Smells, tastes, sounds, sites will never be the same and the Post Traumatic Stress Disorder from my experiences never truly go away. They just stay buried deep until a trigger brings them to the surface. Having been a professional athlete and always an advocate of health and wellness, I live a lifestyle of exercise and healthy eating to prevent diabetes from developing (women with gestational diabetes have a greater chance of developing diabetes later in life.) Healthy eating also helps to strengthen my bones and teeth and I meditate and do yoga on a regular basis to support my mental wellness. I'm proud to say that my last bone scan no longer showed osteopenia and I never had additional cavities.

Knowledge is power

Around the world, there is an expectation that women will experience nausea and vomiting in pregnancy as up to 80% do, but when it overwhelms their body, dramatically reducing the quality of life, most women are left to suffer unnecessarily. Women may lose their job, and the financial strain from this loss of income, in addition to unexpected medical bills is astronomical. Women are told 'this just happens to some women, it is all in their mind, they are looking for attention' or 'they are exaggerating.' There is an unnecessary lack of care causing physical and emotional harm to the mother and baby. Even if it is not intentional, this is not practicing medicine. I have since met women whose organs have failed including; thyroid dysfunction, gallbladder removals, losing their teeth...and I have met countless women whose babies did not make it to full term. In fact some women lose their own lives due to being dismissed and lack of proper medical treatment from their doctors. So that this never happens again. I'm proud to help launch the 'One Mom is Too Many' campaign by the HER Foundation, launched in memory of Maria who died from complications of HG. This is why I know I'm one of the lucky ones!

HG support and Advancements

During my third pregnancy in 2005, I discovered the HER Foundation. Just knowing I was not alone made a world of difference in my mindset! I am forever grateful to the supporters of the HER Foundation for their work as HG Advocates. Although they did not know it at the time, they were instrumental in helping me survive my third HG pregnancy.

Once my youngest daughter was born, I went on with the rest of my life and thought my HG days were behind me. That was not my destiny, however. Since I had volunteered to be part of a HER Foundation's clinical study, (which resulted in Dr. Fejzo, Kimber McGibbon and the rest of their team publishing their results showing the genetic connection of HG) I stayed on their email list. It was an old email address I rarely use, but for some reason checked in the spring of 2019. The subject was "What are you doing for International Gravidarum Awareness Day 2019?" It had been 14 years since I last experienced HG, yet the memories came stinging to the forefront, the feeling of my body shutting down, feeling like I'm dying. If anyone had taken a picture of me when I was pregnant, I would have crushed their camera, but that HER Foundation email had said what hashtags to use when posting on social media. I looked online and saw hundreds of women who are suffering with HG proudly posting pictures of themselves for the world to see. I am grateful to this generation of women proudly putting visuals to the devastating effects of HG because this is what is necessary to create change and revolutionise the way HG women are treated. These images also made me wonder why, with all the amazing scientific advancements, is HG not treated much differently from when I first became pregnant decades ago. Myself and many other women I know were never told by their doctors that they have Hyperemesis Gravidarum. We found out on our own.

I am now armed with knowledge and am proud to say that I educate and train medical practitioners, both outpatient and in the hospitals where I work. I support HG women around the world with treatment options so mum and baby have the best outcomes. I am also a HER Foundation Board Member, host weekly live question and answer sessions on social media and run an HG Consulting business. I currently use an integrative approach and I am always looking for ways to ease HG symptoms without medication, specifically through Nutrigenomics and Epigenetics. I am also currently getting my Doula certification to offer women more support during pregnancy, as having a Doula would have helped me tremendously. I hope that in the near future, we can bio-hack our bodies to prevent HG from taking over. Until that time, I encourage everyone to follow the HER Foundation's medication treatment algorithm and if in the hospital, take charge of your treatment. While we cannot yet treat the cause, we do have options, so trust your gut, ask for help and most importantly, be your own advocate!

I can get through this

"I couldn't function."

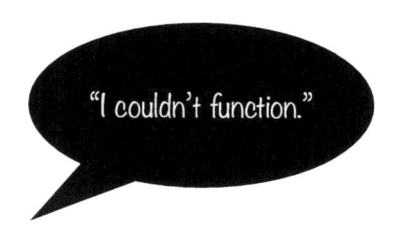

THE HG STORY OF...
CAITLIN

I suffered with HG for the duration of both of my pregnancies with my daughter in 2013/ 2014 and my boy/girl twins in 2017.

Before I became pregnant with my daughter in 2013 I knew nothing about HG. I had heard Princess Kate had been hospitalised for her "bad morning sickness." I remember thinking, how bad could it be? I was wrong to think that. Very wrong. I had a positive pregnancy test at five weeks. My husband and I were so excited to start our family. Three days later the vomiting started and It didn't stop. My GP diagnosed me with HG and started me on medication. I tried all the medication and any tips that had ever been mentioned to help morning sickness (ginger, travel bands, acupuncture, oils, etc.) Ondansetron medication was the only thing that helped me, it limited the vomiting a little. Nothing helped the nausea though, it was relentless. The only time I got relief was when I was sleeping. It was hard to sleep as I was so sick. I couldn't keep anything down apart from the occasional cheeseburger and coke. I had hospital visits for IV fluids and medication.

I kept thinking it would stop after 12 weeks. After 16 weeks, into the third trimester, It still hadn't stopped. I couldn't imagine how it could be worth it. Nothing could be worth being this sick for this long could it? I had to finish work, I couldn't participate in socialising with friends and family. I felt like a zombie, a shell of my usual self. I somehow survived and when our daughter Izzy was born the physical sickness fizzled away. But then the post natal depression and anxiety set in, due to HG. Ladies who have HG pregnancies are at a higher risk of developing perinatal depression and anxiety. It eventually passed and as I got to enjoy my daughter, I realised she was worth all totally worth what I went through.

Could we go through it again

We both desperately wanted another baby and a sibling for Izzy but also knew that I was pretty much guaranteed to get HG again. Could we do this? Could we go through another eight months of hell for the precious reward of another child?

When Izzy was almost three, we decided to try for another baby. Izzy was toilet trained, at preschool, could have sleepovers with grandparents etc. There are amazing mums that do go through HG when their other children are younger but for us it just wasn't an option. This time would be different because I would know what I was in for and I also knew that it would all be worth it! The positive test, again at five weeks, sparked such mixed emotions; excitement and joy for another baby but also fear over what was to come. Again the sickness started three days later. This time it was much worse. I had joined a facebook HG support group and had noticed generally HG seemed to get worse with subsequent pregnancies. My husband commented that maybe as I was sicker it could be twins. My GP said the same and offered a dating scan which I declined.

I was extremely sick. I couldn't work, I couldn't look after Izzy, I couldn't do any of the household tasks. Leaving the house was too hard, I couldn't function. I went from the bed to the bathroom and to the couch. HG is so debilitating, depressing, isolating. I am so lucky to have had a supportive husband and family that could take over looking after Izzy and doing all the household tasks as I couldn't do any of it. Some women with HG don't have that luxury.

I took the Ondansetron and tried to stay as hydrated as I could with small sips of water and hydralyte ice poles. There was no use trying anything else as it didn't work last time and I realised one of the other medications I used last pregnancy had actually been giving me anxiety. I tried to avoid hospital as much as I could this time as I hated it. I only went in for fluids when I had to.

Hyperemesis Gravidarum and twins

Even though it was an informed decision to go through another HG pregnancy, I regretted it when I became sick. Doubt set in, could get through it? I got the details for an abortion. I knew I couldn't go through with that but sadly a proportion of HG pregnancies do end in termination.

Somehow I got through the endless days and nights of vomiting and made it to our 12 week scan. As soon as the ultrasound was on my belly, you could clearly see two babies on the screen! I was so shocked it was twins but my husband of course said "I told you so!"

From there it was just a matter of surviving through each day to the "finish line" and the reward at the end. The daily vomiting, the relentless nausea, the bad headaches, the constipation and other side effects from the Ondansetron. The hospital visits when needed, missing out on life for eight months.

Hyperemesis Gravidarum affects ladies physically and mentally

You know you are lucky to be pregnant and should be grateful and happy but you feel so sick and upset that you have to go through so much suffering that others don't have to. Anger towards the "glowing" pregnant women that sail through pregnancy hits you. You know it will all be worth it and that it will end but the hours, days, months to the finish line all seem so long.

The hours, days, months eventually ticked over and our twins Alexandra and Owen were born at 36 weeks. It was a hectic and challenging birth and recovery for all of us but I felt amazing comparatively and was so ecstatic that they were here and that I didn't have to endure another minute of the living hell of HG! For me, managing newborn twins and an older child was so much easier than dealing with Hyperemesis Gravidarum.

Life after HG

I have had so many people comment and say to me how challenging it must be to have twins (and an older child as well) and that I'm doing a great job but seriously it's so easy compared to surviving through HG. Having twins is such a blessing and to us it feels like we got a bonus child that we never imagined having, as we knew we could only go through another pregnancy. The HG jackpot - two children for one pregnancy! Don't get me wrong of course as any twin mum knows it can be hectic at times but will never compare to the challenge of HG.

The silver lining to come out of my HG experience is that I know I can get through anything! I thought I had faced physical and mental challenges before - I'd lost 30kg, done triathlons, hiked 100km. All were insignificant compared to HG! And of course the amazing "prize" I got at the end of it, our three little ratbags (whoops I mean cherubs!) Our twins are now 3.5 and I'm still reminded of my HG experience almost daily. It's just something I will never forget. I'm passionate about raising awareness and support for women with HG and am always happy to chat with anyone who is experiencing it. I recommend the Australian charity Hyperemesis Australia for resources for HG sufferers and their health care providers. I have had a small involvement with them by doing a fundraising triathlon for their benefit and also being a part of their peer support program.

If you are currently suffering with HG I am truly sorry, I promise you it will all be worth it even though it is hard to imagine it will be. I recommend joining a Facebook HG support group, if you haven't already, as I did find it helpful to know I wasn't alone with my HG struggles.

Tomorrow is another day

"Vomiting up to 30 times a day."

THE HG STORY OF...
ERIN

My pregnancy was not what I expected. I imagined feeling a little sick for a few weeks and then enjoying the rest. Instead, what I experienced was debilitating sickness from four weeks until 24 weeks. I was lucky, my Hyperemesis ended before labour.

I was diagnosed with Hyperemesis Gravidarum when I was seven weeks pregnant. I had been vomiting up to 30 times a day since I was four weeks pregnant. I hadn't moved from my bed in days. I dragged myself to the GP to get help to try and manage. I was told I'd lost 11 kg in two weeks, my blood pressure was high and I was Tachycardic, so I had to take myself to the Emergency department.

That's where I was told to get over it and that it is just morning sickness. Fortunately a nicer, more educated and compassionate doctor saw me and administered fluids over the course of six hours. They also gave me Ondansetron, Maxolon (Metoclopramide) and Doxylamine. I'm lucky that my GP actually prescribed me these medications, not that they did anything. I needed help getting from my bed to the bathroom. I needed help showering because I couldn't stand for that long. I was so sick.

12 weeks in

By the time I was 12 weeks, I had been to the emergency department seven times for fluids and help with constipation, not many people talk about it but when you're so severely dehydrated you get very constipated. Mentally I was so exhausted and termination crossed my mind more than once in the earlier weeks. I remember sitting in the lounge, I was nine weeks pregnant, sick everywhere, hadn't been to the toilet in hours and my partner came home. I just burst into tears, blubbering I don't think I can do this, I feel like I'm dying. And his response was "I was waiting for you to say this, it's ok." That was the lowest I got.

By 14 weeks I could leave the house, but always with my spew bag just in case. By 22 weeks I could leave the house without my spew bag but I always had some Ondansetron on me just in case I needed it. Thankfully by 24 weeks I could go about my day unaffected by my pregnancy. I was lucky.

I will take each day as it comes

> "The sickness was unbearable."

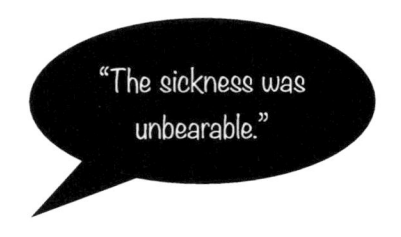

THE HG STORY OF...
GILL

My hg story started when I found out I was seven weeks pregnant with my first child. The sickness was unbearable and continued all day and night. After several days of suffering, I went to the doctors and they gave me some anti-sickness medication. Needless to say It didn't work and by the time I was nine weeks pregnant, I was admitted to hospital and diagnosed with HG. I was given fluids through an IV and more anti-sickness medication. This continued throughout the whole nine months which affected every part of my life. When my first child was 17 months old, I fell pregnant with my second child. To say I was nervous, was an understatement. Once again I went through the same routine of being hospitalised and on IV fluids. It was much harder this time as I had a young child at home. I had to give up work as I was readmitted every other week for three to four days at a time. I was losing so much weight and exhausted by lack of food, sleep and constantly being sick. I felt extremely weak.

Going through another HG pregnancy

After two years, I fell pregnant again but it was horrendous and in the end I ended up terminating the pregnancy as I just couldn't carry on which broke my heart. When my second son was eight, I fell pregnant with my third child. I wouldn't say it was any easier but at least I didn't have toddlers to look after. It was the same old story of being in and out of hospital, but this time was different as I felt like I was a burden on the hospital and some of the staff really didn't understand how serious HG was. It was as if they believed it was just morning sickness, so I really didn't want to be there. I would stay at home and leave it until my veins had collapsed and I was faint and brought up blood.

I didn't think I could get through another HG pregnancy

The strain HG has on your life is hard. Your relationship is strained, you feel like you can't be a mum to your other children. Even some of my own family thought I was just overreacting and would say it was just morning sickness. I had decided to not have any more children as it was too much for my body to take. That was until I met my new partner and we wanted a child of our own. After many months of conversations about this and me explaining about the condition I had and explaining that it wouldn't be easy, we decided to go for it.

In 2017 I had my fourth and final child and wow it didn't get easier. I had tried to convince myself it might. I was admitted into hospital at seven weeks pregnant with dehydration and 4+ ketones. This time I was admitted to another hospital and the staff were amazing and we actually laughed every time I left and they said "see you in a few weeks!" My partner was shocked to see how bad it all was. I ended up having an emergency c-section, three weeks early as my waters broke but he was in the wrong position. All in all I think there should be much more awareness about HG and more support for ladies who are suffering.

The best is yet to come

ABOUT THE AUTHOR

Stefanie Sybens is the author of Letters from the What-Went-Before and the Alliance of Outcasts. She works as a marketing specialist for a tech company and is a freelance web designer for the Real Birth Project. She is currently also finishing a Women's Health and Human Rights course at Stanford University.

She is a HG survivor and founded HG & early motherhood in 2021 to support other women.

Sarah Titmus has survived HG twice. She was born in 1993 in Coventry. She writes poems in her spare time when she isn't doting on her two beautiful girls - Lihanna-Marie and Layla-Mya. Sarah is hoping to publish a poetry book in the new year. Sarah supports student who attend a SEN, specialist, further education college and also volunteers for Pregnancy Sickness Support. Sarah has always been passionate about making a difference to the world, no matter how big or small. Sarah's family and close friends are very important to her, she enjoys spending quality time with them. Sarah also has a love for music and appreciates all genres.

RESOURCES

HG ORGANISATIONS

United Kingdom: Pregnancy Sickness Support
Ireland: Hyperemesis Ireland
Worldwide: HER Foundation
USA: HG pharmacist
Australia: Hypermesis Australia
France: Association de lutte contre l'hyperémèse gravidique
Germany: Hyperemesis Netz
Netherlands: Stichting ZEHG: Zwangerschapsmisselijkheid en Hyperemesis Gravidarum
Denmark: Hyperemesis Danmark
Norway: Hyperemesis Gravidarum Norge
Sweden: Hyperemesis Gravidarum Sverige
Finland: Hyperemeesi ry

MATERNAL MENTAL HEALTH

Maternal Mental Health Alliance
MIND
PANDAS
Samaritans

HG SUPPORT

HG & early motherhood
The Sick film

ANTENATAL SUPPORT

Real Birth Project
Make Birth Better

Printed in Great Britain
by Amazon

Real survivors
Real stories
Real strength

Hyperemesis Gravidarum affects 1-3% of pregnant women and is characterised by severe nausea and vomiting, weight loss, dehydration, ptyalism and a higher chance of mental health issues during and after pregnancy.

Stefanie Sybens and Sarah Titmus have both suffered from this condition and have been avid HG campaigners ever since. They selected stories from other HG sufferers - from all over the world - and brought them to life in this collection.

With this book they hope to support current sufferers during their ongoing HG battle, and be a place of comfort for former HG sufferers who are often forgotten once their journey has ended.

ISBN 9798737400132